lines . from . lindsay

Besides myself, this book is the compilation of 3 very talented scribes... Tamara Sortman, Sande Womack and Ann Wright. Without their beautiful work, this book would not be complete and I thank them ever so much for their incredible style. We added in some styles you have seen before, like the calligraphy and Broadway. However, this time we walked you through exactly how to do them. We think this should give you a little edge on learning the style faster. We also added a color basics section (created by Tamara). Wherever we teach or get to talk to all of you, we constantly get asked how we know what colors go together. Not being a true art teacher, I was not sure how to teach this. We all have worked with color for so long, our combinations just happen. This page is a group effort of some our favorite color basics and we hope you get a lot of use out of them. This book is dedicated to all the friends I am leaving in Southern California. After growing up there and living my over 40 years... my husband and I are moving our family to the sunny blue skies of the California Sierra Nevada Mountains. We are excited to start a new life in a peaceful setting but sad to leave Our Gang! Please e-mail me with any questions or comments at scribbles@earthlink.net..... and please visit my soon to be up and running website at www.seasonalscribbles.com. And remember...... practice, practice, practice !

Happy Scrappin'
Lindsay '99

this . book . belongs . to

D0731388

table . of . contents

❖ Basic Italic ❖

⊛ right handed 45° angle hold.

— the pen goes against this line.

pen tip → goes her

⊛ Lefties who hold their pen from the top of the paper.

⊛ pen hold for lefties who hold their pen like a rightie.

— pen tip goes here.

ok... check out the LMNOP lettering book for all the skinny on the 45° pen hold. Here is a quick guide to all holds, including 3 choices for Lefties. Depending on how you hold your pen, one of these will give you the nice chisled angle you want for a calligraphic look. It's important to get the correct pen hold before you go onto lettering. Pratice zig-zag lines, wavy lines & straight strokes with a good calligraphy pen. 10 minutes per day... it'll happen!

*Basic Italic will help improve all your creative lettering styles. STOP HANDWRITING! START PRINTING!

see the nice chisle tip here? cool!

see how the nice chisle tip comes together here where the "O" lines meet? cool!

Aa Bb Cc Dd

Ee Ff Gg Hh

Ii Jj Kk Ll

Mm Nn Oo Pp

Qq Rr Ss Tt
Uu Vv Ww
Xx Yy Zz
·1234567890·

worksheet

do these exercises before you begin to try real letters!!

zig-zags

wavy gravys

stick stacks

Lefties

(i did this left handed... so it's not so good!)

swish swash

same here- done with my left hand!

this is the part where the teacher says... practice, 10-20 minutes a day or it won't happen. But i'm here to say... that's true — practice, practice, practice... always!!!

Super Calligraphix
Fancy Capitals

A B C D E
F G H I J K
L M N O P Q
R S T U V W
X Y Z

* don't forget all these silly little numbers are the direction your pen/hand goes. when there 2 or 3 #'s, that's the amount of times you pick up your hand to continue ... 2 strokes, 3 strokes!

also... this is where your teacher says... if you really want to learn calligraphy, go to your local parks & rec., or jr. college and take a 3-10 week course. Those teachers are masters!

Lindsay & Brent

see how your capitals & lower case all connect together? Try it yourself ...

•5•

Calligraphix Line-Up

abcdefghijklmnopqrstuvwxyz

1234567890

It's important to practice your lower-case letters in a line... or a circle. Whatever works for placement, line-up and getting the correct 45° angle of the flourishes and serifs. Try placing your paper lengthwise and doing one line and watch for correct connections of all your letters. This is important for making words.

abcdefghijklmnopqrstuvwxyz

try connecting the letters, like th, double j's & t's...

The Breslins

try a fancy flourish on ending letters

pull your higher letters way up & longer letters way down—like p's, y's, j's etc...

try some fun embellishments on your capitals!

Sister Teresa Dodge

this is God's Calligraphic Angel... who taught me calligraphy at 12... Thanks so much

unconventional UNCIAL

A B B C D E
F G H I J K
L M M M N O
P Q R S T U
V U W X Y
Z 1 2 3 4 5 6 7 8 9 0 ; : .

pen tip

pen tip

pen tip
right
handed
45° angle

left
handed
45° angle

pen
tip

lefties who
turn paper

UNCIAL

unconventional

CELTIC

ESQUIRE

happy FATHER'S *day*

WEDDING

GLAMOUR

embellishments

this is one of my favorite things about creative lettering..... taking any style of writing and adding embellishments. Dots, Dashes, triangles, outlines, schwoopies... whatever. So pick your favorite lettering style or make up your own, the let your creative spirit free!!!

add a triangle to the ends of each letter

Aa

add an outline & some slash marks ↓

Bb

Fill in puffed letter with a pattern.

Cc

outline letter with a thin or thick line ↓

Dd

broken line pattern ↓

Ee

put a box around each letter for definition ↘

Ff

add lines & broken lines to look like Kindergarten →

Gg

add a shadow line for extra depth ↘

Hh

shade the dots from thick to thinned out. ↓

Ii

add 2 little quotation lines to show movement →

Jj

Q-Tip style- flair out the ends and add little stitch marks ↗

Kk

add a fancy plaid to the inside of each letter.

Ll

use a white pen and add designs inside. ↗

Mm

add flat lines to the ends of the letters & little lines inside!

Nn

decorate the inside of the letters with fillagree ↘

Oo

Pp **Try adding big blocks where the letters join... great for boys!**

Qq **add graduated lines to the inside of each letter for a ribbon look...**

Rr **add a line of micro dots for a highlight**

Ss **try adding varied slashes for a tire track look**

Tt **add a full outline with stripes inside with a polka dot finish**

Uu **add a dash to dot fade out**

Vv **add some cool geometric designs**

Ww **try a dot & dash varied outline (my new favorite!)**

Xx **add little sticks & stitches inside the letters**

Yy **add some slashes in groups of 2's & 3's....**

Zz **try some long broken lines for shadowing**

put it all together...they spell

MOM

Mother

combine all the styles & techniques.... mix and match them with different lettering styles!

Broadway Basics

...although this style was in my first lettering book...it really didn't teach how to get the lettering done. It took teaching my daughters Fifth Grade Class and the fifth graders telling me how to teach it...to get to this basic alphabet. Do your basic printed alphabet first, then come back (where the dotted line is) to do the fill-in thickening. It's best to outline in pencil while you're learning. This is a great alphabet to fill in with cool patterns——.

ABCDEFG
HIJKLM
NOPQRS
TUVWXYZ
Z

add paterns & designs inside the letters...or shade with colored pencil for a watercolor effect!

Dots   Lines   Checks   Plaids   Swirls

1234567890

lower case basics

a a b c d e
f g h i j k
l m n o p q
r s t u v w
x y z

extra additions

BAILEY

chunky letters
extra slashes
outlined morse code
shapes
overlap with a lower case
flair fill in & outline

longhand

this lettering is done long and low. you want
the letters to be short and flat... and... pulled across
the line as far as possible. Connect all the letters in
the word, and try it with a thin and a thick line.
Also try a little shadow by thickening a portion of the
letter. For a fun title try running the word thru another
word... as shown on the opposit page.

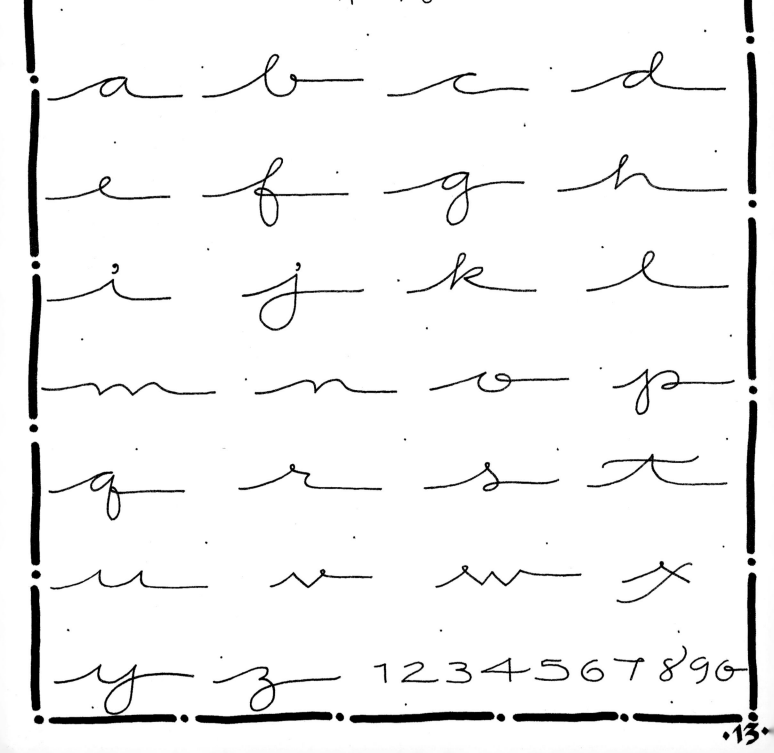

a b c d
e f g h
i j k l
m n o p
q r s t
u v w x
y z 1234567890

long hand

millennium

2000

it's delaney

sunflower

celebrate

this style is dedicated to Michelle Hong... a 6th Grader at Fremont who is a creative lettering queen!

GOT-IT-UP

it's my... Party

Hip Hip HOORAY

You take the Cake

1. write the word Party

2. Outline all the letters in the word. Party

this can be as messy as you want, you're filling it in.

3. how fill in and embellish with outlines & doodles.

Party

Fill·it·Up!

GET OUT YOUR PENCILS, NOT YOUR GAS CARD, BECAUSE THIS FILL UP IS ON US! FOLLOW THESE STEPS AND TRY ALL THE VARIATIONS... I BET YOU'LL COME. UP WITH SOME OF YOUR OWN!

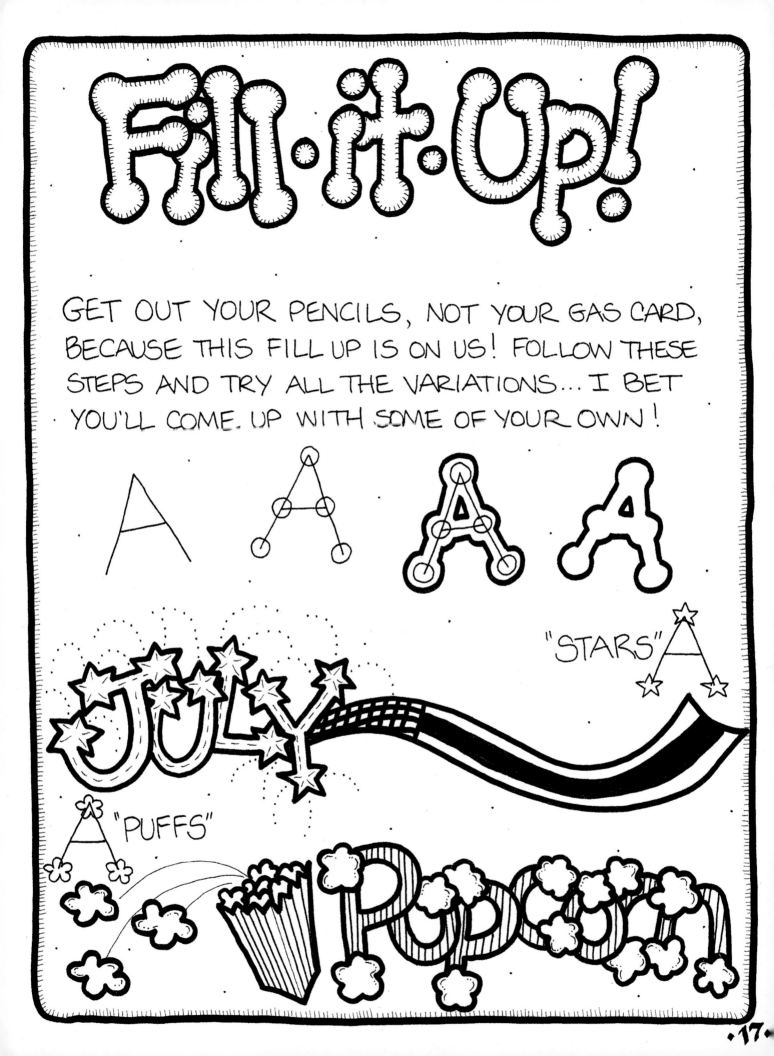

"STARS"

JULY

"PUFFS"

Popcorn

"BLOCKS" A

RODEO

"HEARTS" A

Doggone
BONES

"PUFFS"
ON SCRIPT

Buds

"SPEARS" A

THERE

·18·

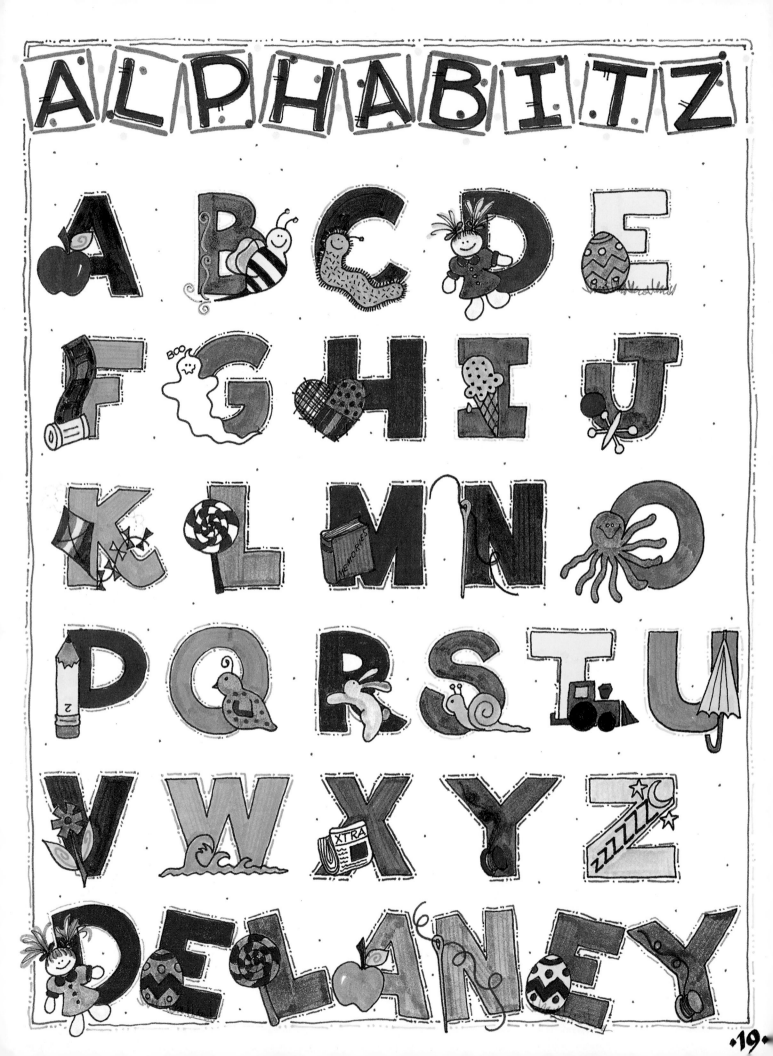

DOLLY
DAISY
DOGGY

great for alphabet books

If you have a light box, trace the letters as is or change the pictures to match your subject. or just use stickers on plain letters.

GHOULS

HEARTS

APPLE · ANIMALS · ANTS · AARDVARK · ALIEN · APE
ABC
BAT · BEAST · BOTTLE · BO
BEE · BOY · BEAVER · BALLOON ·
ALPHABET · AQUATIC · AMORE ·
CAPE · CLAP · CHEER · CASTLE · CAR ·
CATERPILLAR · CAT · CANDLES ·

BOO

MEMORIES

Mother

Checkers

.This is an upper case alphabet that can be used with Broadway caps and lower case. It's also fun to do the checkerboard in colors or filled in with colors. You can outline in black, a color or grey for a shadow. Also, you can take out the flowers and do it plain or with stars and more. Try other patterns inside the letters too. Have fun and be creative......

MOTHER

try a colorful checkerboard.

do some lower case broadway style letters- all slanted with swirls on the ends!

Picnic

try some of the colors from our centerfold of color basics.

also try doing a shadow with a light grey.

from

JULY

People are always asking us how to combine colors and where we get our color combos.
Well — here's a beginning. A sampling. We find colors on bedding, in nature, on
party goods, wallpaper.... wherever. Group your colors in 3's — and try not
like colors. Try odd combonations and you might surprise yourself. Or use
ours shown here — color can make or break your design & lettering —

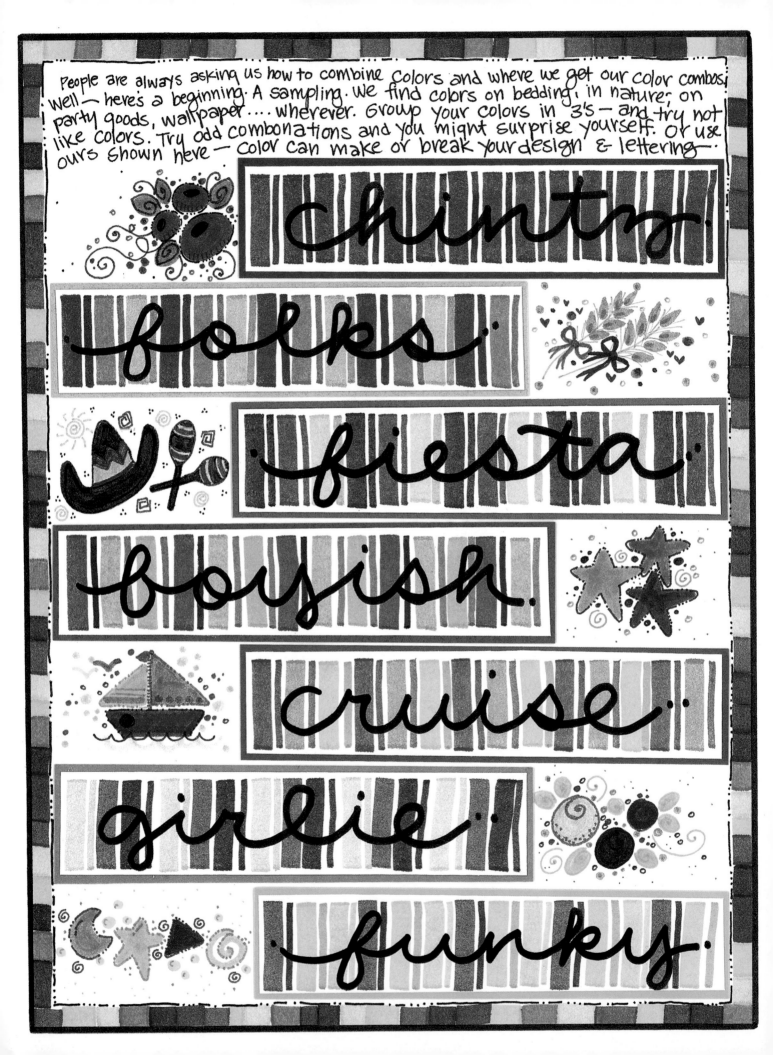

chintz

folks

fiesta

boyish

cruise

girlie

funky

Double Dip

. these next 2 pages show you a cool trick for adding color to any lettering. This is a fast & simple trick to add dazzling depth to your lettering.

Dotz

the lettering is done with a calligraphy pen — in a light shade of blue—.

Do the inside dots in a darker shade of blue—like in the "D" and the "OTZ" were done in the same shade of blue that the lettering was done in — with a fine point pen.

DASHES

this lettering is done with a medium tip pen and is just straight printing with dashes on the ends.
then a darker shade of orange dashes fill the letters.

Diamonds

again... light lettering, darker diamonds to fill-in and then try a cool outline—....

DESIGNS

try this with dark lettering... black, navy, forest, Burgundy etc....

and do your designs with all the new gel, milky & marble pens!

DOO DADS

try a thick chunk lettering...
and do all kinds of designs inside with darker colors & gel pens. This is all fast & simple!

buzz

to put some buzz in your words try your lettering in one color & stripe it in another. Try it with 2 similar tones... Like pink on pink etc......

and add in little doo-dads too!

BUBBLES

do a thick lettering, like broadway or puff and fill it in with a wave and some way cool little bubbles!!!

Baroque

try doing a thick handwritten word and filling in with swirls...

finish it off with an outline & some mini dots...

BOO!

basically beautiful... Boo is done in the same technique as the "buzz" up above...try it in red & green for Christmas too!!!

Berries

Do some big and bold broadway letters in a rose color and then add 1 shade darker dot inside. This makes a berry quick and tasty little style !!!

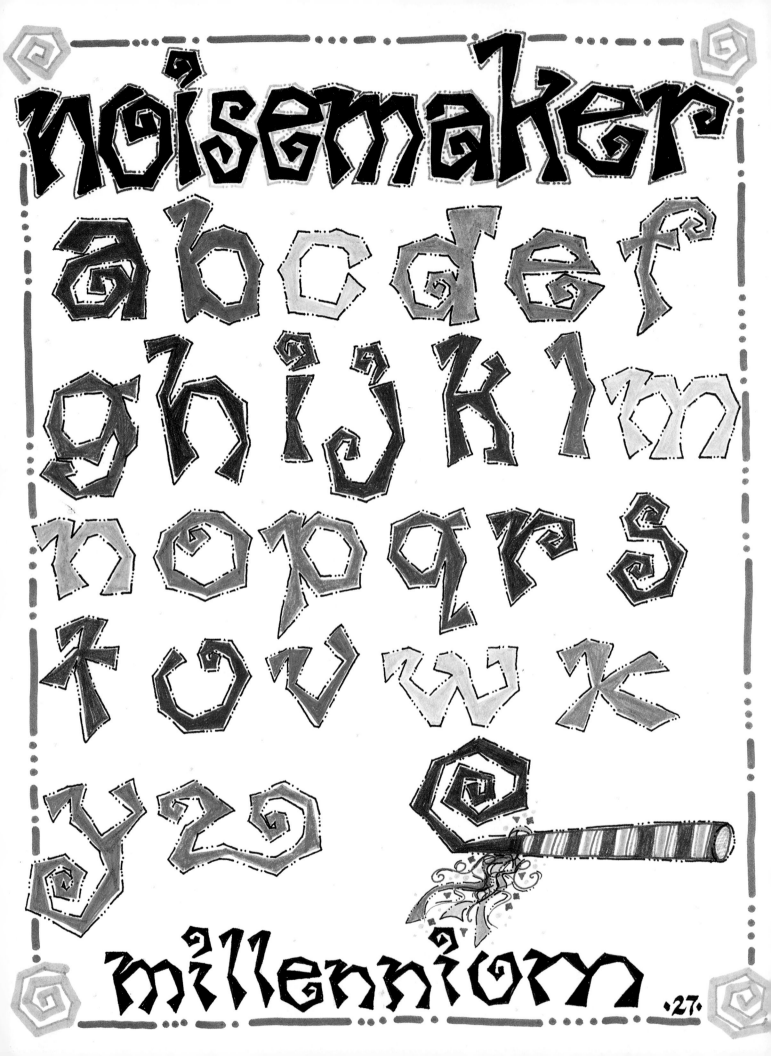

noisemaker

a b c d e f
g h i j k l m
n o p q r s
t u v w x
y z

millennium

·27·

new year celebration

joyful vicry carnival

1. write the word
2. do elongated triangles in different directions. Think of the octagonal shape of a stop sign.
3. now fill it in with pen and outline in whatever color you like.

fun
fun
fun

STOP 4 FUN

·28·

A B C D E

F G H I J

K L M N O

P Q R S T

U V W X Y Z

Scrapramento ABCs

this lettering got it's name from my friend Tamara's web site (www.scrapramento.com). when you do this, set each letter on an angle or slant. And get creative with the design fillings for each letter. Check out our website!

SURF ON OVER

come on, let's...

SCRAP!

Try doing your own lettering styles too and mix and match the letters

DOOFUS

this is a lettering style with very few rules. basically.... you do your writing, kinda up & down — not to straight and add a thick part to one area of the letter.

CALIFORNIA

try adding a triangle to the ends of each letter.... COOL!

now.... add some fun doo-dads to the insides of the letters —— have fun!

Aa Bb
Cc Dd Ee
Ff Gg Hh

I i J j K k

L l M m N n

O o P p Q q

R r S s T t

U u V v W w

X x Y y Z z

32

CHUNK

IT'S SO EASY! JUST START WITH A SQUARE, OR A CIRCLE! I USED THE SQUARE FROM THE "BIRTH-DAY" RULE-IT-UP RULER AND THE CIRCLE FROM THE "BASICS" RULE-IT-UP. JUST TRACE THE SHAPE WITH A PENCIL, SKETCH IN YOUR LETTER AND INK IT IN! ERASE YOUR PENCIL LINES WITH A WHITE ERASER LIKE "ERASE-IT-UP"!

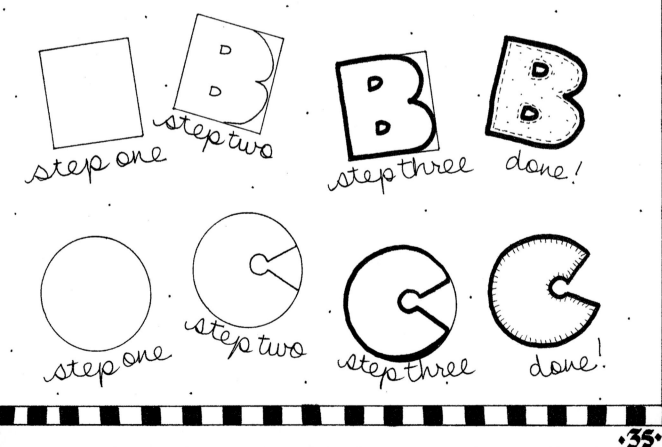

step one step two step three done!

step one step two step three done!

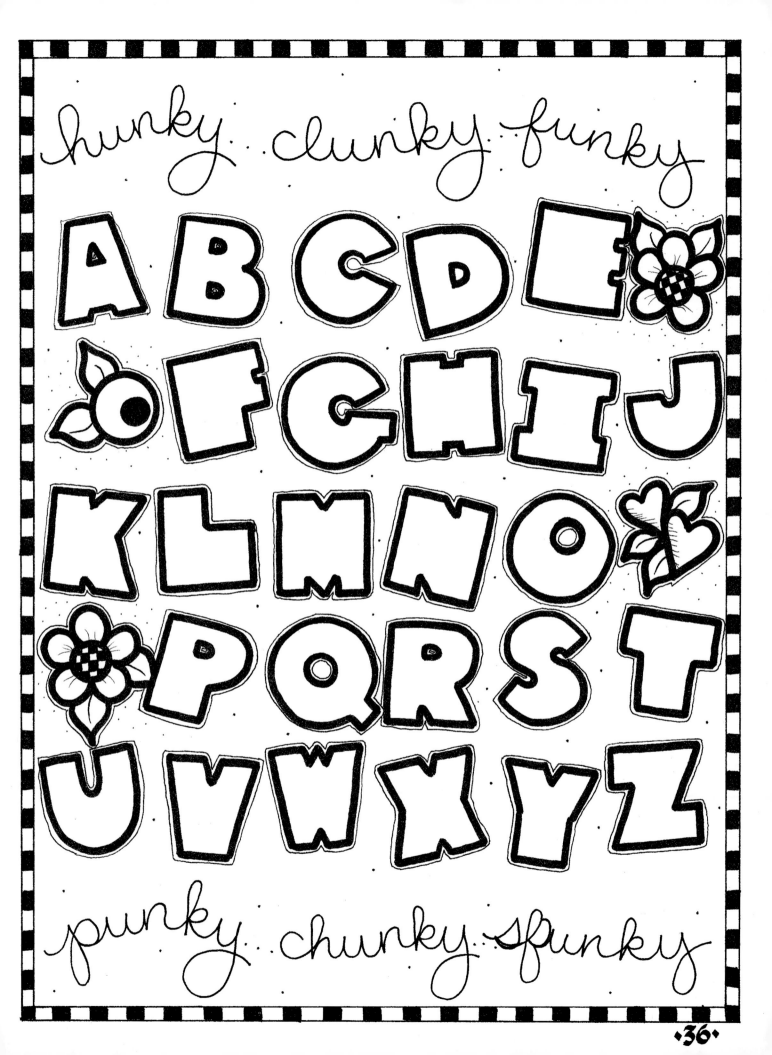

Splish Splash

this alphabet is wonderful for all kinds of invitations, scrapbook pages, banners and more. Try it in color and with a dash of glitter for that extra little splash——....

Aa Bb Cc Dd Ee

Ff Gg Hh Ii Jj Kk

Ll Mm Nn Oo Pp

Qq Rr Ss Tt Uu

Vv Ww Xx Yy Zz

0 1 2 3 4 5 6 7 8 9

Splish Splash

SWIM TEAM

this lettering is so fun to do in color as well as black and white. Try the letters in black and the bubble splashes in Light Blue, Green, Turquoise and try mixing the colors together with colored pencil or a blending pen.

also try using glitter in the splashes. Use an ultra fine prisma glitter over a clear liquid glue. The end result will be bubbly and full of sparkles.

my first bath

1. Draw a simple printed letter.

2. Bubble-Up the ends and fasten the lines.

3. color in the bubbles and add splashes.

Chop Stix

A a B b C c D d E e
F f G g H h I i J j
K k L l M m N n O o P p
Q q R r S s T t U u
V v W w X x Y y Z z

0 1 2 3 4 5 6 7 8 9

Chop Stix

shopping in...

China Town

With all the traveling we are doing it's fun to add a little culture to our words. Try this with some cool tips from color basics ——*

Kitty

our vacation in...

Beijing
1448

1.
A
Z

Pencil in long adjoining triangles.

2.
A
Z

Outline with pen. Let dry. then erase pencil lines.

3.
A
Z

Fill in solid or embellish.

Congratulations

you have successfully completed

Creative Lettering

What are you waiting for? Now go home and practice, practice, practice........

·TEACHER·

·D·A·T·E·